My Dog Jimmy
The Story of a Good Boy and Parents 'n' Puppies

CHRISTINA RAMPELLINI
PATRICIA RAMPELLINI

Copyright © 2023
Christina Rampellini
Patricia Rampellini

Performance Publishing
McKinney, TX

All Worldwide Rights Reserved.
All rights reserved. No part of this publication may be reproduced, stored in a retrieval system or transmitted, in any form or by any means, electronic, mechanical, recorded, photocopied, or otherwise, without the prior written permission of the copyright owner, except by a reviewer who may quote brief passages in a review.

ISBN: 978-1-961781-12-2

PRAISE FOR *MY DOG JIMMY*

"*My Dog Jimmy* is an engaging tale of a girl and her dog. I give it 5 out of 5 wagging tails."

— Mary Rampellini, Correspondent & Handicapper
Daily Racing Form

"*My Dog Jimmy* is a wonderful children's book about the heartwarming relationship between the author and her beloved dog, Jimmy. From Jimmy's puppy days to his adventures through the years, this book offers valuable life lessons and insight into the importance of family bonds and unconditional love. The inclusion of real photos, alongside the beautifully blended paintings, adds a unique and engaging touch to the story. It's an engaging tale for readers of all ages."

— Michelle Prince, CEO
Prince Performance Group, LLC
www.MichellePrince.com

"It is a sweet book."

— Marianna Folger
Private Piano Teacher

Bark at Us! Please send a testimonial or constructive criticism to: cmerjmj@yahoo.com

For the Lord.

For my Dad, Mom, and
Family, for all they do.

For the Education Department at
the University of Dallas, and
Dr. Melissa Caraway, Elementary Education;
Dr. Robert Alexander, English,
Literary Tradition II,
and Dr. Jo Ann Patton, High
School Education

For all who contributed to the making of this book, including:

Michelle Prince & the team at Performance Publishing Group: Carlo Angelo Tuvila (cover designer), John Hirayama (book interior designer), Nancy Acevedo (project manager), Jennifer Hart (communications & collaboration)

Mary Rampellini, John & Ellen Arnott and Ronnie.

And for Jimmy – and all dogs and cats!

On Easter morning in the year 2002, six puppies were born on an out-of-state trip to Arkansas.

Our family dog, Janie,
was the happy mother.

Annie (brown, closest), Ralph (brown, right), and Jimmy (tan and white, far right)!

The best part was naming the puppies and seeing each of their personalities when they played.

There were five boys.

Annie was the only girl, and you could tell Janie really cared for her in a special way.

One day, a neighborhood friend came over.
She was excited to see the puppies!

But Janie, being a protective mother,
nipped at our neighbor.
It was kind of scary.

Thankfully, our neighbor was
okay. (She was tough!)
Dad tended to the neighbor's ouchie.
But I learned a lesson...

Don't let anyone see a mom
and her puppies!
Because anyone could get nipped.
Janie is a happy — but protective
— mother around other people.

As the puppies grew, we had to decide which puppy to keep, because we couldn't take care of all of them.

My Mom was very influential in making this decision. She said she did like Jimmy because of his clean, white fur. So, with Mom's approval, my family and I knew Jimmy was the one to keep.

We gave the five other puppies away to other families.

Coco, a Portuguese swimmer, is
Jimmy's dad. He lives in Arkansas.

Janie, a miniature Australian shepherd, is
Jimmy's mom. She lives in Oklahoma.

Coco and Janie are happy,
quiet, and well-behaved.

Jimmy has become very
special to our family.

Every morning, we let Jimmy out into the backyard. Sometimes, Jimmy plays with his dog friend along the back fence.

He barks and races back and forth. Then he rests his front paws up against the wood of the fence before he takes off running again.

Jimmy not only likes to bark when he is playing with his dog friend, he also enjoys barking at squirrels scurrying along the fence, and armadillos, possums, and frogs. If anyone comes over to our house to visit, Jimmy will also bark.

After Jimmy plays in the backyard, we let him inside for his breakfast.

Jimmy seems to have acquired a taste for crunchy dog food.

He likes that the best, and he always drinks water.

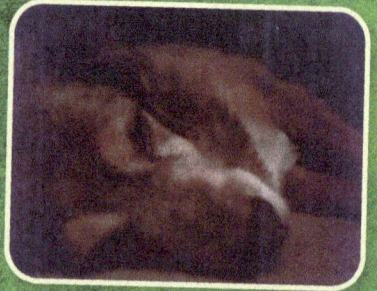

After Jimmy rests during the day, he loves to go for a walk.

When we put his leash on him, he heads right to the front door.

He means business.

When the fall weather comes, we put Jimmy's brown dog coat on him.

My mom made it.

Like he does with my mom, Jimmy also has a special connection with my dad. On Sunday mornings after church, and at dinner, too, he sits patiently, waiting for a piece of toast or some little treat from my dad.

So, that's my dog Jimmy, from Arkansas to our home in Texas. He is still and will always be a puppy at heart, just eight and a half years older now!

ABOUT THE AUTHOR

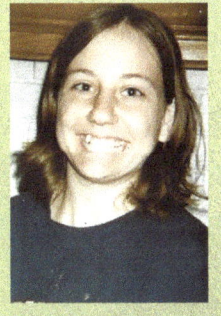

Christina Rampellini resides in Dallas/Fort Worth and is the youngest of four children. Her older siblings are Mary, Anna, and Ralph. Her parents are Pat and Ralph Rampellini, and her dog is Jimmy!

Christina is a graduate of Church Preschool, Northwest ISD, and the University of Dallas, and aspires to become an elementary school teacher one day. Christina also holds an Accounting Clerk certificate from Dallas College and has studied online marketing and advertising.

The author has spent time working in the education, public service, and restaurant industries. She enjoys going to church with her family, playing the piano and guitar, volunteering, and playing basketball and tennis. Christina enjoys her mom's homemade pizza and hamburger soup. She loves going to the beach in Galveston with her family.

The author currently has a pet sitting service in Dallas/Fort Worth. For those services, or copies of *My Dog Jimmy* for classrooms, libraries, or your own collection, please email: cmerjmj@yahoo.com

ABOUT THE ILLUSTRATOR

Patricia Rampellini kindly contributed to the making of this book through her illustrations. Aside from being a wonderful mom to her family, she loves painting cards and stationery, candles, and sewing. She learned how to sew at a young age and her family enjoys her cooking, especially during the holidays.

www.ingramcontent.com/pod-product-compliance
Lightning Source LLC
Chambersburg PA
CBHW040323050426
42453CB00018B/2446